Lectin Free Meal Prep

Easy and Fast Lectin Free Meal Prep Recipes for Beginners (Reduce Inflammation, Lose Weight and Prevent Disease)

Frank Roberts

© Copyright 2018 Frank Roberts- All Rights Reserved.

In no way is it legal to reproduce, duplicate, or transmit any part of this document by either electronic means or in printed format. Recording of this publication is strictly prohibited, and any storage of this material is not allowed unless with written permission from the publisher. All rights reserved.

The information provided herein is stated to be truthful and consistent, in that any liability, regarding inattention or otherwise, by any usage or abuse of any policies, processes, or directions contained within is the solitary and complete responsibility of the recipient reader. Under no circumstances will any legal liability or blame be held against the publisher for any reparation, damages, or monetary loss due to the information herein, either directly or indirectly.

Respective authors own all copyrights not held by the publisher.

Legal Notice:

This book is copyright protected. This is only for personal use. You cannot amend, distribute, sell, use, quote or paraphrase any part of the content within this book without the consent of the author or copyright owner. Legal action will be pursued if this is breached.

Disclaimer Notice:

Please note the information contained within this document is for educational and entertainment purposes only. Every attempt has been made to provide accurate, up-to-date and reliable, complete information. No warranties of any kind are expressed or implied. Readers acknowledge that the author is not engaging in the rendering of legal, financial, medical or professional advice.

By reading this document, the reader agrees that under no circumstances are we responsible for any losses, direct or indirect, which are incurred as a result of the use of information contained within this document, including, but not limited to, errors, omissions, or inaccuracies.

Table of contents

CHAPTER 1: UNDERSTANDING THE LECTIN FREE DIET 7
    What are Lectins? 7
    What is wrong with Lectins? 10

CHAPTER 2: WHY MEAL PREP? 11
    Benefits of Meal Prepping 11

CHAPTER 3: THE COMMON MISTAKES BY MEAL PREPPING BEGINNERS 13

CHAPTER 4: FOODS TO EAT 15

CHAPTER 5: FOODS TO AVOID 16

CHAPTER 6: TIPS 17
    Tips on Lectin Free Diet 17
    Tips on Meal Prepping 17

CHAPTER 7: BREAKFAST RECIPES 18
    Carrot Bread 18
    Flourless Bread 20
    Coconut Cereal 21
    Korean Style Steamed Eggs 22
    Egg Muffins 23
    Fruity Nutty Milkshake 24
    Green Goddess Smoothie 25
    Fruits and Veggie Breakfast Bowl 26

CHAPTER 8: SNACKS RECIPES 27
    Chicken Nuggets 27
    Kale Chips 29
    Mini Cucumber Bites 30
    Crunchy Almond Honey Bark 31

Crispy Sweet Potato Chips 32

Chocolaty Nuts 33

Avocado Snack 34

Traditional Yummy Cookies 35

CHAPTER 9: FISH AND SEAFOOD RECIPES 36

Shrimp Salad 36

Omega-Rich Salmon 38

Delightful Salmon Burgers 39

Lemon Filled Trout 41

Salmon and Asparagus 42

Trout BBQ Party 44

Tangy and Sweet Salmon 45

Tuna with Avocado 47

CHAPTER 10: POULTRY RECIPES 48

Chicken Thighs 48

Aromatic Turkey Drumsticks 50

Chicken Legs with Carrots 51

Turkey and Brussels Sprouts 52

Indian Roasted Chicken 54

Thanksgiving Turkey 56

MEAT RECIPES 57

Harvest Beef Salad 57

Bright Colored Beef Burgers 59

Family Dinner Pork Shoulder 60

Hawaiian Pineapple Pork 61

Delish Lamb Chops 63

Prime Rib Roast 65

Beef and Cauliflower 66

Divine Leg of Lamb 68

Superior Beef Tenderloin Roast 70

Mushroom Beef Steaks 71

CHAPTER 11: VEGETABLES RECIPES 73

Veggies-filled Mushrooms 73

Citrus Brussels Sprout 75

Crispy Veggie Salad 76

Hearty Broccoli 78

Sweet & Sour Kale 80

Cauliflower Patties 81

Colorful Beet Pesto 83

Tropical Fruity Salad 85

CHAPTER 12: DESSERTS RECIPES 86

Pumpkin Brownies 86

Strawberries Chia Seeds Pudding 87

Grilled Peaches 88

Blueberry Cake 89

Chocolate Mousse 90

Strawberry Custard 91

Berry Granita 92

Dark Chocolate Fudge 93

CONCLUSION 94

CHAPTER 1: UNDERSTANDING THE LECTIN FREE DIET

There are two types of lectins that are known to be problematic to the humans. The first type of lectins is called prolamins. Gluten is an example of prolamins, as they contain rich content of amino acids. The second type of lectins is called agglutinin. Kidney beans are an example of agglutinins. Following will help you understand the lectins better.

What are Lectins?

Lectins are principally those proteins which have the responsibility of binding cell membranes together. They are having a sugar binding nature and are actually the 'glyco' section of the glycoconjugates existing on the cell membranes. It supports the cells to join together without the help of the immune mechanism. It is credited as the compulsory element for intercellular bindings.

Lectins comprises of a considerable amount of raw grains and legumes and is ordinarily present in that exceptional part of the seed i.e. cotyledon, which converts into the leaves after the sprouting and growth of the plant. It is to note hereby that the quantity of lectins in the food is roughly constant but with the arrival of cross breeding and different genetic and biological experimentation have caused the amount of lectins to differ from plant to plant.

Lectin proteins are found in the foods such as plants, grains and beans. They tend to bind with the carbohydrates which can help communicate the cells to interact with each other. They are the proteins that cause inflammation and weight gain and they are found in plants. Lectins are found in many foods and they are ubiquitous in nature. Lectins might get disabled by the use of some specific monosaccharides and oligosaccharides. They bind to ingest lectins from the grains, nightshade plants. They prevent them from binding with the carbohydrates and hence are useful for neutralizing lectins.

The most efficient way of eliminating or lowering down the quantity of lectins in plants are those cooking processes which work in moist heat. The starches in plants are substantially and effectually fragmented down into carbohydrates by cooking which are much simpler in nature. Lectins are associated to these carbs, which are then befittingly taken out of the human body prior to their detrimental and undesirable impacts and effects. The reason for not having a preference to slow cooking for the preparation of kidney beans is the fact that the lower temperature is being effective enough for the exclusion of lectins. The most effective and well-suited ways for the removal of lectins are elucidated as follows:

- Peeling

Peeling is a procedure that involves the removal of skin, peel or husk of various fruits, vegetables and grains that possess lectins.

- Deseeding

Deseeding is a procedure that involves the elimination of seeds from various lectin possessing fruits and vegetables. After the removal of the seeds, the fruits and vegetables become free of lectin, as the seeds contain most of the lectin proteins.

- Boiling

Boiling the lectin-carrying fruits and vegetables, like tomatoes, remove the remaining lectins from them.

- Fermentation:

Fermentation is a procedure that comprises of consenting advantageous bacteria for the human body which is effective in digestion and transmuting different harmful substances into safe ones. This is the motive for the wide usage of fermented soy substance i.e. natto, tamari, tempeh and miso by many healthy people across the world. Vegetables like cabbage, etc. after fermentation carry minor quantities of anti-nutrients. Those entities who have objections regarding intake of grains have considered applying the procedure of fermentation for treating grains. This technique is one way or another effective in elimination of lectins, but it is stated that a few hardcore natured lectins are not influenced by the process of fermentation.

- Sprouting:

The quantity of lectins is significantly lowered in beans, grains and seeds after they are sprouted. This procedure is highly effective if the sprouting is performed over a longer time span. In certain rare cases the amount of lectins and their effectiveness is increased after sprouting (considering the case of alfalfa). The seed coats of certain seeds and grains contain lectins, when they are germinated, the coating is metabolized and this results in the removal of lectins.

- Pressure cooking and Soaking:

The sole factor for boiling, rinsing and soaking of beans is reducing the amount of lectins present in them. This process has been adapted for since a long time now and has somehow proved to be effective. Beans and legumes are soaked overnight and the water is repeatedly changed for the effective removal of lectins present in them. On top of this, addition of baking soda to the soaking water can enhance the effects of removing lectins from the beans.

There are many benefits of lectins too in addition to its harmful effects. A smaller quantity of lectins is considered to be beneficial for the bacteria which are present in the human digestive system. According to a scientific research, lectins are well-thought-out to be very effective for the diagnosing and identification of cancer. A research is being carried out which sheds light for the role of lectins in discontinuing cancer cells from multiplying. They are many studies being conducted by medical experts and scientists for the role of lectins in playing a defensive mechanism, remedy and even as a treatment against various medical complications and ailments which are instigated by several fungi, bacteria and viruses.

What is wrong with Lectins?

Lectins are identified to be adversely affecting health in definite ways. This ranges from attaining the risks of certain chronic illnesses to complications and medical condition concerning gastrointestinal system of the human body. They are well-thought-out to be the cause for the clustering of red blood cells. They are also observed to be anti-nutrients for their function in halting the digestion and absorption of numerous nutrients. They are also attributed to be the reason for triggering digestive ailments in circumstances when plant related foods are not cooked appropriately or at all prior to their consumption. They are also credited for the harmful effects caused by legumes which are not properly cooked.

The lectins are tough to digest and they have an effect providing them the ability of over-feeding a few strains of gut bacteria, leading to gut dysbiosis. The gut dysbiosis is linked to variety of health conditions and are certainly not good for health.

They have an ability to interact with the gut barrier and can cause some serious damage to the cells that form the gut barrier or worse they can cause is to open up the junctions between the cells. Of course, the genetic susceptibility plays a big role in how your body reacts to this or what happens in your body. They are big contributors to the development of a leaky gut which is linked to a variety of health conditions.

The lectin found plentifully in red beans is 'Phytohemagglutinin', which is remarkably recognized for triggering 'red kidney bean poisoning', a medical complication possessing the symptoms of vomiting, nausea and even severe form of diarrhea. The red kidney bean poisoning is initiated by eating undercooked or raw kidney beans. According to the findings, research and statement of United States Food & Drug Administration (FDA), a mere amount of '04' kidney beans are enough to result in red kidney bean poisoning if they are consumed in undercooked or raw form.

CHAPTER 2: WHY MEAL PREP?

The process of preparing all or some of the meals for a certain period of time prior to the time of their consumption is called meal prepping. You will be preparing all your meals yourself that you see on the television or social networking platforms without any processed ingredients. But in case of meal prepping, you will be personally preparing all these recipes and provide yourself with the most delicious, nutritious and healthy foods without any processed ingredients.

Meal prepping has been gaining fame amongst millions of people and these numbers are increasing by leaps and bounds. The reason is that the hectic routines of people make this plan convenient and effective as it is pretty much money and time saving but also gives you a platform to have nutritious, tasty food from time to time. Meal prepping also prevents you from the hazards of canned, processed and packaged foods which possess highly injurious amounts of calories and pose a serious threat to our health.

Benefits of Meal Prepping

Meal prepping can be useful because you prepare your food first and then that healthy food will never let you go for the canned food which has many disoriented ingredients in it that can harm your body. Meal prepping can make preparing anything in a larger quantity, preparing a bunch of vegetables or even making many whole meals for an occasion and then freezing all or some of it for the later use. It might mean that you would take some time for washing the vegetables or chopping them for the dinner made plans which happen suddenly or using them for later. You can also prepare something which you are preparing already but that has to be in a bigger amount so that you can use it when you are not feeling well or when you are too tired to prepare anything or even if your plans are not working properly.

Meal prepping and meal planning work as a couple to guarantee the efficiency of your plan. They provide you the food of your choice with the most healthiest and nutritious ingredients ever. Meal planning responds to the interrogations about what to have at a certain meal time for consumption while meal prepping essentially delivers the answer to your query. In the absence of meal planning, meal prepping will be more complex and too hard to adopt. Meal prepping is the practical accomplishment of your meal planning by clutching the mandatory ingredients and items involved in the recipes you opted for prepping your meals for the coming week or so.

CHAPTER 3: THE COMMON MISTAKES BY MEAL PREPPING BEGINNERS

The mistakes that the meal prepping beginners make are fairly common and are very easily to be dealt with. One mistake is very often seen and that is not giving oneself not sufficient time for planning. No matter how long you have spent the time on the meal but the planning takes time and it does not happen in a morning or in one afternoon. The solution for that would be give yourself enough time to plan especially when you are getting started. Setting aside three to four hours each day for a week for meal planning would do the job. Take advantage of the weekend and plan and prep for the meal.

The other mistake that is often seen is not picking the right recipe for your needs. In order to make the meal planning work for you, you have to know the right needs about the recipe. When you pick the recipe that fit your criteria, you are left hungry, frustrated and unsatisfied. To overcome this problem you have to pick the meals that are suitable for your gut. Even before you go out and search for a recipe always right down what do you actually want with a recipe and clear your head with it.

The other problem is quite unforeseen and happens to almost everyone. That is being overly ambitious and unrealistic. You have to remember that meal prepping is not a sprint it is a marathon. It is great to feel so enthusiastic and inspired about the meal planning but making one that is overly unrealistic and does not quite match your needs or your schedule to work with it will not do. It will never be sustainable in the long run. You can start by assessing your schedule and making your goals that what exactly suits you and at what time you can work the best at it. If you are having doubts about that, there is absolutely no problem, start small, start making once or twice in a week. Gradually you will overcome this situation.

Another problem often seen is that people do not scout the kitchen for food that needs to be used up. Do not ever forget to shop your own kitchen for the leftover food that needs to be used up. Take advantage of the leftover ingredients you have already made use of. It is a fairly simple step that can help you prevent waste of food and maybe you can even save a little money with that. So what you should do, you should scout the pantry and the fridge before you head out to the store. You surely will find something that will save you some money or it can maybe save you a whole trip.

This is a very big blunder and people make it so often. It is so important to overcome that it should be made a sin. It is not saving or writing down the recipes. When you organize the things, you are more likely to get the best out of the ingredients and not doing that makes you vulnerable for something bad to happen. Organization is the key for the perfect meal. Not writing down your recipes makes you falls off the track and it is hard to get back on it. Always remember to jot down the effort you are putting in the food. It has to be something that you write in a saved diary or something that you will not lose.

This problem happens to armature of the field and happens a lot. They cook new recipes each and every night. Cooking new recipes is great and it should be like this but we should go about this strategically. Filling whole of the week with new recipes is quite thrilling and ambitious but it is also unrealistic. It will prove to be overwhelming and unsustainable in the long run. Do not try all new recipes at the same time, rather give each one its due time and dignify it by giving yourself and that recipe some space. Build most of your week with the recipes you know and then add one at a time in the week that you are not very mature at.

CHAPTER 4: FOODS TO EAT

According to the findings made by Dr. Gundry, following are the foods that are recommended and are considerably befitting for those individuals who are interested to control their lectin intake and limit the consumption of carbohydrates joining foods in an effective manner:

- A-2 milk
- Green and leafy vegetables
- Cooked potatoes
- Meats which are pasture rose
- Onions
- Garlic
- Celery
- Asparagus
- Vegetables which are cruciferous in nature which are Brussles sprouts and Broccoli
- Olives and extra virgin olive oil
- Mushrooms
- Avocado

CHAPTER 5: FOODS TO AVOID

Apart from the foods that help to lower the levels of lectins in the body, there are also such foods which are high on the lectins and one should avoid eating them. According to the findings done by Dr. Gundry the following are the foods to avoid for the individuals who are looking forward to decrease the amount of lectins in their body:

- Nightshade vegetables like peppers, potatoes, eggplants and tomatoes
- Legumes such as beans, lentils, peanuts
- Grain. If it is necessary to consume grains, Dr. Gundry has recommended the use of white flour instead of wheat in them
- Squash
- Only in seasoned foods are allowed to be consumed otherwise the fruits as a whole are not recommended in lectin free diet plan.

Some foods have strictly not been recommended for the individuals who are looking forward to decreasing their lectin level because these are high on the lectin and they will cause serious damage

- Corn
- Meats from the animals who are fed on corn
- A-1 milk

CHAPTER 6: TIPS

Tips on Lectin Free Diet

Online stores and wholesale clubs are the best alternative for the lectin free shopping list. To avoid making it a financial burden, always divide your shopping list into groups to avoid any extra financial burden. Do not forget to prefer white grains over brown grains because brown grains have lectins in them in a large amount and they are not recommended for lectin free diet plan. Always remember to peel your fruit and deseed it before eating. Use a pressure cooker when you plan to cook a lectin free meal. Consuming natural foods will make it easier for you to drop lectins like extra virgin olive oils, leafy greens, olives, avocados, cruciferous vegetables.

Tips on Meal Prepping

Considering a few tips, for time saving in rush mornings, you can prepare and freeze smoothies for a week to avoid getting late for your office or college. You can try going for a better freezer or refrigerator to prep effectively. You can go for taco meats, fajita fillings, soups, breakfast burritos, egg muffins and so much more for meal prepping. You can chop your vegetables, cook grains in a larger amount for addition and have already prepared proteins for making your lunch get on your table in a go.

CHAPTER 7: BREAKFAST RECIPES

Carrot Bread

Preparation Time: 15 minutes
Cooking Time: 35 minutes
Servings: 6
Ingredients:
- 1 teaspoon ground cinnamon
- 2 tablespoons coconut flour
- 3 organic eggs
- ½ cup carrots, peeled and shredded
- 1 teaspoon organic baking powder
- ¼ teaspoon salt
- 1/3 cup organic honey
- ¼ cup walnuts, chopped
- 2 cups almond flour
- 1 teaspoon baking soda
- ¼ cup coconut oil, melted

Method:
1. Preheat the oven to 340 degrees F and grease a loaf pan with cooking spray.
2. Mix together coconut flour, baking soda, baking powder, cinnamon and salt in a mixing bowl.
3. Combine carrots, eggs, honey and coconut oil in another bowl.
4. Combine both the mixtures slowly and top with walnuts.
5. Transfer the mixture into prepared loaf pan and bake for about 35 minutes.

Meal Prep Tip: Place the bread slices in a reseal able plastic bag and seal the bag after squeezing the excess air. Keep the bread away from direct sunlight and preserve in a cool and dry place for about 2 days.

Nutritional Value:
- Calories 439
- Total Fat 32.3 g
- Saturated Fat 10.2 g

- Cholesterol 82 mg
- Total Carbs 27.5 g
- Dietary Fiber 5.8 g
- Sugar 16.2 g
- Protein 12.5 g

Flourless Bread

Preparation Time: 10 minutes
Cooking Time: 35 minutes
Servings: 6

Ingredients:

- 1½ teaspoons baking soda
- 5 organic eggs
- 1½ cups cashew butter
- 1½ tablespoons apple cider vinegar
- 1 teaspoon salt

Method:

1. Preheat the oven to 420 degrees F and grease a loaf pan with cooking spray.
2. Add all the ingredients in a blender and pulse until smooth.
3. Transfer the mixture into prepared loaf pan and bake for about 35 minutes.
4. Remove from the oven and keep aside to cool and serve.

Meal Prep Tip: Place the bread in a resealable plastic bag and seal the bag after squeezing the excess air. Keep the bread away from direct sunlight and preserve in a cool and dry place for about 2 days.

Nutritional Value:

- Calories 430
- Total Fat 35.3 g
- Saturated Fat 7.4 g
- Cholesterol 136 mg
- Total Carbs 18 g
- Dietary Fiber 1.3 g
- Sugar 0.3 g
- Protein 15.9 g

Coconut Cereal

Preparation Time: 10 minutes
Cooking Time: 25 minutes
Servings: 8

Ingredients:
- 1 teaspoon ground nutmeg
- ½ teaspoon stevia powder
- 1 tablespoon ground cinnamon
- 1 tablespoon organic vanilla extract
- ½ cup filtered water
- 1-pound unsweetened coconut flakes

Method:
1. Preheat the oven to 340 degrees F and line 8 baking sheets with parchment paper.
2. Put together all the ingredients in a bowl until well mixed.
3. Transfer this mixture into prepared baking sheets and bake for about 25 minutes.
4. Dish out and transfer this cereal into an airtight container.

Meal Prep Tip: Transfer this cereal into an airtight container and preserve in refrigerator for about 1-2 weeks.

Nutritional Value:
- Calories 279
- Total Fat 22.8 g
- Saturated Fat 19 g
- Cholesterol 0 mg
- Total Carbs 17.5 g
- Dietary Fiber 8.1 g
- Sugar 1.5 g
- Protein 3.9 g

Korean Style Steamed Eggs

Preparation Time: 5 minutes
Cooking Time: 7 minutes
Servings: 6

Ingredients:
- 1 teaspoon sesame seeds
- 1½ cups cold water
- 1 teaspoon garlic powder
- 1 teaspoon salt
- 6 large pasture eggs
- 6 teaspoons scallions, chopped
- 1 teaspoon black pepper

Method:
1. Whisk together eggs and water in a bowl and strain this egg mixture over a fine mesh strainer.
2. Put water in the cooker pot and arrange a steamer rack in it.
3. Put the egg bowl over the steamer rack and secure the lid.
4. Cook for about 7 minutes at high pressure.
5. Naturally release the pressure and carefully remove the rack.

Meal Prep Tip: Transfer the steamed eggs into airtight container and refrigerate for up to 3 days. Reheat in microwave before serving.

Nutritional Value:
- Calories 76
- Total Fat 4.8 g
- Saturated Fat 1.5 g
- Cholesterol 215 mg
- Total Carbs 1.9 g
- Dietary Fiber 0.3 g
- Sugar 0.2 g
- Protein 6.3 g

Egg Muffins

Preparation Time: 10 minutes
Cooking Time: 12 minutes
Servings: 6

Ingredients:

- 6 grass-fed bacon slices, precooked
- 1½ teaspoons lemon pepper seasoning
- 1½ green onions, diced
- 6 eggs
- 2 cups water

Method:

1. Whisk together all the ingredients in a large mixing bowl.
2. Pour the muffin batter in muffin moulds equally.
3. Put water in the cooker pot and arrange a steamer rack in it.
4. Transfer these muffins on the rack and secure the lid.
5. Cook for about 12 minutes at high pressure.
6. Naturally release the pressure and carefully remove the muffins.

Meal Prep Tip: Invert the muffins carefully onto a wire rack to cool completely. Line 2 airtight containers with paper towels and arrange muffins over paper towel in a single layer. Cover muffins with another paper towel and refrigerate for about 2-3 days. Reheat in the microwave on High for about 1½ minutes before serving.

Nutritional Value:

- Calories 145
- Total Fat 10.4 g
- Saturated Fat 4.4 g
- Cholesterol 179 mg
- Total Carbs 1 g
- Dietary Fiber 0.2 g
- Sugar 0.4 g
- Protein 10.7 g

Fruity Nutty Milkshake

Preparation Time: 15 minutes
Cooking Time: 0 minute
Servings: 6
Ingredients:
- 6 tablespoons chia seeds
- 8 tablespoons almonds, chopped
- 4 cups unsweetened almond milk
- 2 teaspoons ground cinnamon
- 4 cups frozen strawberries

Method:
1. Put all the ingredients in an immersion blender.
2. Pulse until smooth and pour into serving glasses.

Meal Prep Tip: Divide all ingredients in 2 containers except almond milk. Cover and store in freezer for about 3 days. Remove containers from freezer just before serving and transfer into a blender with almond milk and pulse until smooth.

Nutritional Value:
- Calories 245
- Total Fat 15 g
- Saturated Fat 1.4 g
- Cholesterol 0 mg
- Total Carbs 24.2 g
- Dietary Fiber 13.8 g
- Sugar 6.3 g
- Protein 7.1 g

Green Goddess Smoothie

Preparation Time: 10 minutes
Cooking Time: 0 minute
Servings: 6
Ingredients:
- 3 cups fresh baby kale
- 6 cups romaine lettuce, chopped
- 12 tablespoons fresh lemon juice
- 6 cups filtered water
- 1 cup fresh mint leaves
- 2 cups ice cubes
- 3 large avocados, peeled, pitted and chopped
- 3 cups fresh collards
- 3 drops liquid stevia

Method:
1. Put water and all the other ingredients in an immersion blender and pulse until smooth.
2. Pour into 6 serving glasses to serve immediately.

Meal Prep Tip: Divide all ingredients in 2 containers except ice cubes and stevia. Cover and store in freezer for about 3 days. Remove containers from freezer just before serving and transfer into a blender with ice cubes and stevia and pulse until smooth.

Nutritional Value:
- Calories 200
- Total Fat 11.4 g
- Saturated Fat 3.4 g
- Cholesterol 13 mg
- Total Carbs 20.6 g
- Dietary Fiber 5.5 g
- Sugar 10.3 g
- Protein 7.6 g

Fruits and Veggie Breakfast Bowl

Preparation Time: 15 minutes
Cooking Time: 0 minute
Servings: 6

Ingredients:

- 6 tablespoons cacao powder
- 3 large green bananas
- ¾ cup wild blueberries
- 3 cups cauliflower, chopped finely
- 6 tablespoons cacao nibs
- 1/3 cup unsweetened almond milk
- 3 tablespoons almond butter

Method:

1. Put cauliflower, almond milk, banana, cacao powder and almond butter in a blender.
2. Pulse until smooth and transfer the mixture into serving bowl.
3. Top with blueberries and cacao nibs and serve.

Meal Prep Tip: Transfer this cereal into an airtight container and preserve in refrigerator for 1-2 weeks.

Nutritional Value:

- Calories 283
- Total Fat 12.2 g
- Saturated Fat 4.6 g
- Cholesterol 0 mg
- Total Carbs 42.5 g
- Dietary Fiber 16.4 g
- Sugar 11.5 g
- Protein 8.8 g

CHAPTER 8: SNACKS RECIPES

Chicken Nuggets

Preparation Time: 15 minutes
Cooking Time: 12 minutes
Servings: 6
Ingredients:
- 1 cup almond flour
- 3 (6-ounce) pasture-raised chicken breasts, skinless, boneless and pounded
- ¾ cup coconut flour
- 3 organic eggs
- ¾ teaspoon garlic powder
- Salt and freshly ground black pepper, to taste
- ¾ teaspoon dried oregano, crushed
- ¾ teaspoon dried thyme, crushed
- ¾ teaspoon smoked paprika

Method:
1. Preheat the oven to 390 degrees F and grease a baking sheet.
2. Cut the chicken into equal sized nuggets and whisk eggs in a shallow dish.
3. Combine together almond flour, coconut flour, garlic powder, herbs, paprika, salt and black pepper in another large dish.
4. Dip each nugget in whisked eggs and then dredge in the flour mixture.
5. Arrange chicken nuggets onto baking sheet and bake for about 12 minutes.

Meal Prep Tip: Remove the nuggets from heat and keep aside to cool completely. In 4 containers, divide nuggets evenly and refrigerate for about 2 days. Reheat in microwave before serving.

Nutritional Value:
- Calories 297
- Total Fat 13.8 g
- Saturated Fat 2.4 g
- Cholesterol 131 mg
- Total Carbs 14.8 g

- Dietary Fiber 8.3 g
- Sugar 0.3 g
- Protein 28.5 g

Kale Chips

Preparation Time: 15 minutes
Cooking Time: 12 minutes
Servings: 6

Ingredients:
- ¾ teaspoon garlic powder
- 6 cups fresh kale leaves, stalks removed and torn into large pieces
- 1½ tablespoons avocado oil
- 1/3 teaspoon red chili powder
- Salt, to taste
- 1/3 teaspoon ground cumin
- 2 tablespoons nutritional yeast
- ¼ teaspoon cayenne pepper

Method:
1. Preheat the oven to 320 degrees F and grease a baking sheet.
2. Pat dry the kale pieces with paper towel and add in a bowl along with half of oil.
3. Sprinkle with spices and 1 tablespoon of nutritional yeast.
4. Add remaining oil to the kale leaves and arrange the kale pieces onto the prepared baking sheet.
5. Sprinkle with remaining nutritional yeast and salt and bake for about 12 minutes.

Meal Prep Tip: Place the kale chips in a resealable plastic bag and seal the bag after squeezing the excess air. Preserve in a refrigerator for about 2 days. Microwave on high for about 1 minute before eating.

Nutritional Value:
- Calories 52
- Total Fat 0.7 g
- Saturated Fat 0.1 g
- Cholesterol 0 mg
- Total Carbs 9.2 g
- Dietary Fiber 2.1 g
- Sugar 0.1 g
- Protein 3.7 g

Mini Cucumber Bites

Preparation Time: 15 minutes
Cooking Time: 0 minute
Servings: 6

Ingredients:
- 1/3 cup coconut cream
- 2 cucumbers, peeled and deseeded, cut crosswise into ¾-inch thick slices
- 2 tablespoons fresh chives, minced
- ounce cooked salmon, very finely chopped
- Salt and freshly ground black pepper, to taste
- 2 tablespoons shallots, minced
- 1/3 teaspoon smoked paprika

Method:
1. Put all the ingredients in a bowl except cucumber and toss to coat well.
2. Arrange the salmon mixture over each cucumber slice and immediately serve.

Meal Prep Tip: Transfer these mini cucumber bites into an airtight container and preserve in refrigerator for about 3 days.

Nutritional Value:
- Calories 124
- Total Fat 6.8 g
- Saturated Fat 3.4 g
- Cholesterol 25 mg
- Total Carbs 5.1 g
- Dietary Fiber 0.9 g
- Sugar 2.2 g
- Protein 12.1 g

Crunchy Almond Honey Bark

Preparation Time: 12 minutes
Cooking Time: 40 minutes
Servings: 6

Ingredients:
- ½ cup organic honey
- 1 cup unsalted almonds
- ½ teaspoon salt
- 1 cup unsweetened coconut flakes

Method:
1. Preheat the oven to 330 degrees F and grease a baking dish.
2. Put coconut, salt, maple syrup and almonds in a large bowl.
3. Stir to combine and arrange the almond mixture into prepared baking dish.
4. Bake for about 40 minutes and invert the bars on a rack.
5. Cut into equal sized bars and serve.

Meal Prep Tip: Transfer these barks into an airtight container and preserve in refrigerator for about 2 weeks.

Nutritional Value:
- Calories 224
- Total Fat 11.9 g
- Saturated Fat 3.9 g
- Cholesterol 0 mg
- Total Carbs 29.3 g
- Dietary Fiber 3.4 g
- Sugar 23.9 g
- Protein 4.1 g

Crispy Sweet Potato Chips

Preparation Time: 15 minutes
Cooking Time: 25 minutes
Servings: 6

Ingredients:

- 1/3 cup olive oil
- 1½ pounds sweet potatoes, peeled and cut into paper-thin rounds
- Salt, to taste

Method:

1. Preheat the oven to 400 degrees F and grease baking sheets.
2. Put oil and sweet potato rounds in a large bowl and shake to coat well.
3. Arrange the sweet potato rounds onto prepared baking sheets and season lightly with salt.
4. Bake for about 25 minutes and dish out.

Meal Prep Tip: Place the kale chips in a resealable plastic bag and seal the bag after squeezing the excess air. Preserve in a refrigerator for about 2 days. Microwave on high for about 2 minutes before eating.

Nutritional Value:

- Calories 230
- Total Fat 11.4 g
- Saturated Fat 1.6 g
- Cholesterol 0 mg
- Total Carbs 31.6 g
- Dietary Fiber 4.7 g
- Sugar 0.6 g
- Protein 1.7 g

Chocolaty Nuts

Preparation Time: 10 minutes
Cooking Time: 0 minute
Servings: 7

Ingredients:
- 1/3 cup flaxseeds
- 1 cup raw pecans
- 1/3 cup 75% chocolate chips
- 1 cup raw cashews
- ¼ teaspoon salt
- 1 cup raw walnuts

Method:
1. Add all the ingredients in a bowl and toss to coat well.
2. Transfer into an airtight container and preserve at room temperature.

Meal Prep Tip: Transfer these chocolaty into an airtight container and preserve in refrigerator for about 2 weeks.

Nutritional Value:
- Calories 278
- Total Fat 23.6 g
- Saturated Fat 3.3 g
- Cholesterol 2 mg
- Total Carbs 11.4 g
- Dietary Fiber 3.5 g
- Sugar 2.6 g
- Protein 8.7 g

Avocado Snack

Preparation Time: 15 minutes
Cooking Time: 20 minutes
Servings: 4

Ingredients:
- 1½ teaspoons fresh lime juice
- ¼ teaspoon cayenne pepper
- Salt, to taste
- 4 large organic eggs, boiled, peeled, yolks removed and sliced in vertical halves
- ¾ medium avocado, peeled, pitted and chopped

Method:
1. Put avocado, lime juice, egg yolks and salt in a bowl and mash with a fork.
2. Scoop the avocado mixture evenly in the egg halves and dust with cayenne pepper.

Meal Prep Tip: Put all the avocado snacks in resealable bags and refrigerate for about 2 days. Reheat in microwave before serving.

Nutritional Value:
- Calories 153
- Total Fat 12.4 g
- Saturated Fat 3.1 g
- Cholesterol 186 mg
- Total Carbs 5.1 g
- Dietary Fiber 2.6 g
- Sugar 0.9 g
- Protein 7.1 g

Traditional Yummy Cookies

Preparation Time: 15 minutes
Cooking Time: 12 minutes
Servings: 9

Ingredients:

- ¼ cup organic honey
- ¼ cup arrowroot powder
- 1½ cups almond flour
- ¼ cup coconut oil, melted
- ¼ cup unsweetened coconut, shredded

Method:

1. Preheat the oven to 345 degrees F and grease a baking dish.
2. Mix together all the ingredients in a bowl except coconut to make dough.
3. Make equal sized balls from the dough and coat each ball evenly with coconut.
4. Arrange the balls onto a cookie sheet and press each ball gently.
5. Bake for about 12 minutes and invert the cookies onto wire rack.

Meal Prep Tip: Transfer these cookies into an airtight container and store for about 2 weeks.

Nutritional Value:

- Calories 216
- Total Fat 0.3 g
- Saturated Fat 0 g
- Cholesterol 0 mg
- Total Carbs 15.7 g
- Dietary Fiber 2.2 g
- Sugar 7.9 g
- Protein 4.1 g

CHAPTER 9: FISH AND SEAFOOD RECIPES

Shrimp Salad

Preparation Time: 20 minutes
Cooking Time: 9 minutes
Servings: 4

Ingredients:
For Salad:
- 4 cups fresh baby spinach, chopped
- 1½ cups fresh bok choy, trimmed
- 1½ avocados, peeled, pitted and cubed
- Salt and freshly ground black pepper, to taste
- 2 cups fresh mango, peeled, pitted and chopped
- 1½ tablespoons fresh lime juice
- 2 garlic cloves, minced
- ¼ cup extra-virgin olive oil

For Shrimp:
- ¾ teaspoon dried rosemary, crushed
- 3 medium garlic cloves, peeled
- Salt and freshly ground black pepper, to taste
- 1½ tablespoons fresh lime juice
- ¾ pound shrimp, peeled and deveined
- 1½ tablespoons olive oil

Method:
1. For Salad: Cook bok choy for about 3 minutes in a pan of salted boiling water.
2. Drain well and transfer into a large bowl.
3. Stir in remaining salad ingredients and divide the salad in serving plates.
4. For Shrimp: Put all the ingredients in a large bowl except shrimp.
5. Coat the shrimp in this mixture and refrigerate to marinate for about 2 hours.
6. Preheat the oven broiler and arrange the rack in upper position.
7. Grease a baking sheet and transfer the shrimp onto prepared baking sheet.
8. Broil for about 3 minutes on each side and transfer the shrimp mixture in a bowl and refrigerate to cool.

9. Add shrimp mixture to the salad and toss to coat well.
10. Serve immediately.

Meal Prep Tip: Divide salad in 4 containers and refrigerate for about 1 day.

Nutritional Value:
- Calories 437
- Total Fat 29.3 g
- Saturated Fat 5.5 g
- Cholesterol 179 mg
- Total Carbs 26 g
- Dietary Fiber 7.6 g
- Sugar 12.7 g
- Protein 23.1 g

Omega-Rich Salmon

Preparation Time: 15 minutes
Cooking Time: 16 minutes
Servings: 6

Ingredients:
- 3 tablespoons fresh lemon juice
- 3 garlic cloves, minced
- 1½ tablespoons fresh lemon zest, grated finely
- 6 (6-ounce) skinless, boneless salmon fillets
- Salt and freshly ground black pepper, to taste
- 3 tablespoons olive oil

Method:
1. Preheat the grill and grease the grill grate.
2. Put all the ingredients in a large bowl except salmon fillets.
3. Dredge the salmon fillets in this mixture and arrange on the grill grate.
4. Grill the salmon steaks for about 8 minutes on each side to serve.

Meal Prep Tip: Transfer the salmon steaks into airtight containers by placing parchment papers in between. Cover the containers and refrigerate for about 1 day. Reheat in the microwave before serving.

Nutritional Value:
- Calories 280
- Total Fat 13.2 g
- Saturated Fat 3.3 g
- Cholesterol 99 mg
- Total Carbs 1.8 g
- Dietary Fiber 0.4 g
- Sugar 0.5 g
- Protein 38.3 g

Delightful Salmon Burgers

Preparation Time: 20 minutes
Cooking Time: 17 minutes
Servings: 8
Ingredients:
- 3 tablespoons fresh parsley, chopped
- 18-ounce slightly cooked salmon
- ¾ cup onion, minced
- ¾ teaspoon paprika
- 3 tablespoons olive oil
- 1 garlic cloves, minced
- Salt and freshly ground black pepper, to taste
- 4 organic egg yolks

Method:
1. Preheat the oven to 345 degrees F and grease a large baking sheet.
2. Put all the ingredients in a large bowl except oil and make equal sized patties from the mixture.
3. Arrange patties onto prepared baking dish and bake for about 15 minutes.
4. Heat oil in a large skillet and transfer the salmon burgers in it.
5. Cook for about 1 minute on each side and serve hot.

Meal Prep Tip: Remove the patties from heat and keep aside to completely cool. Store in an airtight container and in order to avoid sticking, place parchment papers in between the burgers. These burgers can be stored in the freezer for up to 1 month. Thaw the burgers before serving and reheat in microwave.

Nutritional Value:
- Calories 162
- Total Fat 11.5 g
- Saturated Fat 2.1 g
- Cholesterol 133 mg
- Total Carbs 1.7 g
- Dietary Fiber 0.4 g
- Sugar 0.5 g

- Protein 13.9 g

Lemon Filled Trout

Preparation Time: 15 minutes
Cooking Time: 27 minutes
Servings: 6

Ingredients:
- 3 fresh dill sprigs
- Salt and freshly ground black pepper, to taste
- 3 lemons, seeded, sliced thinly and divided
- 3 whole rainbow trout, gutted and cleaned
- 3 tablespoons olive oil
- 3 fennel bulbs, sliced

Method:
1. Preheat the oven to 495 degrees F and grease a baking dish.
2. Arrange the fennel slices in the bottom of the baking pan.
3. Season each trout with salt and black pepper.
4. Stuff the cavity of trout with dill sprigs and half of lemon slices.
5. Layer the fish over the fennel slices and top with remaining lemon slices.
6. Drizzle with olive oil and bake for about 15 minutes.
7. Lower the temperature of oven to 430 degrees F and bake for about 12 more minutes.

Meal Prep Tip: Remove the trout from oven and keep aside to cool completely. Store in an airtight container and store in the freezer for up to 3 weeks. Reheat in the microwave before serving.

Nutritional Value:
- Calories 281
- Total Fat 12.7 g
- Saturated Fat 2.4 g
- Cholesterol 81 mg
- Total Carbs 11.5 g
- Dietary Fiber 4.5 g
- Sugar 0.7 g
- Protein 31.6 g

Salmon and Asparagus

Preparation Time: 15 minutes
Cooking Time: 20 minutes
Servings: 6

Ingredients:
- 1½ tablespoons fresh dill, minced
- 6 garlic cloves, peeled and minced
- 6 tablespoons coconut aminos
- 6 tablespoons scallion (green part), chopped
- 6 (4-ounce) boneless salmon fillets
- 3 tablespoons fresh lemon juice
- 1½ pounds asparagus, trimmed and cut into 2-inch pieces
- 3 tablespoons olive oil
- Salt and freshly ground black pepper, to taste

Method:
1. Preheat the oven to 345 degrees F and grease a large piece of foil.
2. Place asparagus in the centre of foil and arrange salmon fillets on it.
3. Mix together dill, oil, lemon juice, garlic, coconut aminos, black pepper and salt in a bowl.
4. Pour this mixture over asparagus and salmon fillets.
5. Bake for about 20 minutes and garnish with scallions.

Meal Prep Tip: Transfer the salmon mixture into a large bowl and keep aside to cool completely. Divide the mixture into 6 containers and cover the containers. Refrigerate for about 1 day and reheat in the microwave before serving.

Nutritional Value:
- Calories 258
- Total Fat 14.3 g
- Saturated Fat 2.1 g
- Cholesterol 50 mg
- Total Carbs 9.4 g
- Dietary Fiber 2.7 g
- Sugar 2.5 g

- Protein 25 g

Trout BBQ Party

Preparation Time: 15 minutes
Cooking Time: 6 minutes
Servings: 6

Ingredients:
- 3 lemons, sliced thinly and divided
- 1½ large onions, sliced thinly
- 3 garlic cloves, crushed
- 3 tablespoons olive oil
- 9 rainbow trout fillets
- Salt and freshly ground black pepper, to taste

Method:
1. Preheat the grill to medium-high heat and grease the grill grate.
2. Rub the trout with garlic and arrange each trout slice over a piece of foil.
3. Arrange the lemon slices and onions over fillets and sprinkle with salt and black pepper.
4. Drizzle with olive oil and fold the foil pieces to seal the trout slices.
5. Grill the trout for about 6 minutes and serve hot.

Meal Prep Tip: Remove the trout from grill and keep aside to cool completely. Store in an airtight container and store in the freezer for up to 1 month. Reheat in the microwave before serving.

Nutritional Value:
- Calories 281
- Total Fat 19.1 g
- Saturated Fat 4 g
- Cholesterol 68 mg
- Total Carbs 11.2 g
- Dietary Fiber 1.6 g
- Sugar 3.8 g
- Protein 20.3 g

Tangy and Sweet Salmon

Preparation Time: 15 minutes
Cooking Time: 17 minutes
Servings: 6

Ingredients:
- 6 (6-ounce) fresh salmon fillets
- ¾ tablespoon red pepper flakes, crushed
- ¼ teaspoon ground cinnamon
- ¾ cup organic honey
- ¾ cup scallions, chopped
- Salt and freshly ground black pepper, to taste
- 3 teaspoons extra-virgin olive oil, divided
- 1½ tablespoons fresh lemon juice
- ¾ cup coconut aminos

Method:
1. Put all the spices in a large bowl, mix well and keep aside.
2. Add salmon fillets, lemon juice and half of the oil to this spice mixture and toss to coat well.
3. Allow it to refrigerate for at least an hour.
4. Mix together honey and coconut aminos in a pan and place over medium heat.
5. Cook for about 10 minutes, occasionally stirring.
6. Heat remaining oil in a large skillet over high heat and add salmon fillets.
7. Cook for about 4 minutes and carefully flip the sides, glazing with honey.
8. Cook for about 3 minutes and transfer the fillets in serving plates.
9. Top with the glaze from pan and garnish with scallions.

Meal Prep Tip: Transfer the salmon fillets into airtight containers by placing parchment papers in between. Cover the containers and refrigerate for about 1 day. Reheat in the microwave before serving.

Nutritional Value:
- Calories 411
- Total Fat 13 g
- Saturated Fat 1.9 g

- Cholesterol 75 mg
- Total Carbs 42.4 g
- Dietary Fiber 0.7 g
- Sugar 35.2 g
- Protein 33.5 g

Tuna with Avocado

Preparation Time: 15 minutes
Cooking Time: 10 minutes
Servings: 6

Ingredients:
- 3 tablespoons onion, chopped finely
- ounce cooked tuna
- 3 large avocados, halved and scooped out the flesh from middle
- 6 tablespoons fresh lemon juice
- Salt and freshly ground black pepper, to taste

Method:
1. Mash avocado and onions in a bowl and top with lemon juice.
2. Stir in tuna, salt and black pepper and divide this mixture in both avocado halves.

Meal Prep Tip: Transfer the tuna filled avocado into 6 containers evenly and cover the containers. Refrigerate for about 2 days and reheat in the microwave before serving.

Nutritional Value:
- Calories 273
- Total Fat 18.8 g
- Saturated Fat 3.1 g
- Cholesterol 21 mg
- Total Carbs 8.3 g
- Dietary Fiber 6.1 g
- Sugar 0.8 g
- Protein 19.4 g

CHAPTER 10: POULTRY RECIPES

Chicken Thighs

Preparation Time: 15 minutes
Cooking Time: 1 hour
Servings: 4
Ingredients:
- 3 cups homemade chicken broth
- ½ teaspoon cayenne pepper
- ¾ tablespoon filtered water
- 4 grass-fed bone-in chicken thighs
- 1½ tablespoons extra-virgin olive oil
- 1/3 onion, sliced
- 5 fresh rosemary sprigs
- 1½ tablespoons fresh lemon juice
- 1½ tablespoons arrowroot starch
- 1/3 tablespoon fresh lemon zest, grated finely
- Salt and freshly ground black pepper, to taste

Method:
1. Season the chicken thighs with salt and black pepper and heat oil over high heat in a large skillet.
2. Put the chicken, skin side down and cook for about 4 minutes.
3. Dish out the thighs onto a plate and add onions in the same skillet with broth.
4. Sauté for about 5 minutes and return the thighs in the skillet.
5. Top with rosemary sprigs and cayenne pepper.
6. Bring to a boil and reduce the heat to medium-low.
7. Simmer, covered for about 45 minutes, coating the thighs with cooking liquid.
8. Meanwhile, mix together arrowroot starch and water in a small bowl.
9. Remove the rosemary sprigs and transfer the thighs into a bowl.
10. Pour the lemon juice in sauce and stir to combine.
11. Add arrowroot starch mixture and cook for about 4 minutes.
12. Pour this sauce over dished out chicken thighs and top with lemon zest.

Meal Prep Tip: Transfer the chicken thighs into a large bowl and keep aside to cool completely. Divide the mixture into 4 containers evenly. Cover the containers and refrigerate for up to 4 days. Reheat in the microwave before serving.

Nutritional Value:
- Calories 335
- Total Fat 23.6 g
- Saturated Fat 6.2 g
- Cholesterol 95 mg
- Total Carbs 5.5 g
- Dietary Fiber 1 g
- Sugar 1.1 g
- Protein 23.9 g

Aromatic Turkey Drumsticks

Preparation Time: 15 minutes
Cooking Time: 45 minutes
Servings: 6

Ingredients:

- 1½ teaspoons dried thyme
- 1/3 cup olive oil
- Salt and freshly ground black pepper, to taste
- 1½ teaspoons paprika
- 1½ teaspoons dried rosemary
- 6 (10-ounce) pasture-raised turkey drumsticks, bone-in, skin-on
- 1½ teaspoons garlic powder

Method:

1. Preheat the oven to 440 degrees F and grease a rack arranging in a roasting pan.
2. Mix together spices and herbs in a bowl and drizzle the turkey drumsticks with the oil.
3. Dredge in the herb mixture and arrange the turkey legs over the rack in roasting pan.
4. Roast for about 30 minutes and wrap the roasting pan with a piece of foil.
5. Roast for about 15 minutes and dish out to keep aside for about 10 minutes.

Meal Prep Tip: Divide the turkey mixture evenly in 6 containers and refrigerate for about 2 days. Reheat in microwave before serving.

Nutritional Value:

- Calories 547
- Total Fat 20.5 g
- Saturated Fat 4.6 g
- Cholesterol 196 mg
- Total Carbs 1.2 g
- Dietary Fiber 0.5 g
- Sugar 0.2 g
- Protein 85 g

Chicken Legs with Carrots

Preparation Time: 15 minutes
Cooking Time: 40 minutes
Servings: 6

Ingredients:
- 6 (6-ounce) pasture-raised chicken legs
- 3 pounds carrots, peeled and sliced
- 3 tablespoons olive oil
- Salt and freshly ground black pepper, to taste
- 1½ tablespoons dried rosemary, crushed

Method:
1. Preheat the oven to 395 degrees F and grease a large baking dish.
2. Arrange carrot slices in the bottom of prepared baking dish and top with chicken legs.
3. Sprinkle with salt, black pepper and rosemary evenly and drizzle with oil.
4. Roast for about 40 minutes, tossing once after 20 minutes.

Meal Prep Tip: Divide the chicken mixture into 6 containers and cover them. Store in refrigerator for up to 1 week and reheat before serving.

Nutritional Value:
- Calories 475
- Total Fat 28.4 g
- Saturated Fat 7.1 g
- Cholesterol 144 mg
- Total Carbs 24.4 g
- Dietary Fiber 5.9 g
- Sugar 11.2 g
- Protein 32.3 g

Turkey and Brussels Sprouts

Preparation Time: 15 minutes
Cooking Time: 1 hour 30 minutes
Servings: 12

Ingredients:

For Turkey Breast:
- 3 tablespoons olive oil
- 3 teaspoons paprika
- Salt and freshly ground black pepper, to taste
- 3 (3-pound) turkey breast halves, bone-in and pasture-raised

For Brussels Sprouts:
- 3 pounds fresh Brussels sprouts
- 1½ tablespoons olive oil
- Salt and freshly ground black pepper, to taste

Method:
1. Preheat the oven to 435 degrees F and grease a large roasting pan.
2. Rub the breast halves generously with salt, paprika and black pepper and sprinkle evenly with olive oil.
3. Place turkey breast halves in prepared roasting pan and put it in the oven.
4. Decrease the temperature to 365 degrees F and roast for about 1½ hours.
5. Remove from the oven and cut the breast halves in desired slices.
6. Meanwhile, boil Brussels sprouts in a large pan and cook for about 20 minutes.
7. Drain the Brussels sprouts well and dish out into a large bowl.
8. Add remaining ingredients and toss to coat well.
9. Split Brussels sprouts in serving plates and top with breast slices.

Meal Prep Tip: Divide the turkey slices with Brussels sprouts evenly in 9 containers and refrigerate for about 4 days. Reheat in microwave before serving.

Nutritional Value:
- Calories 436
- Total Fat 14.2 g
- Saturated Fat 2.6 g
- Cholesterol 170 mg

- Total Carbs 10.6 g
- Dietary Fiber 4.5 g
- Sugar 2.5 g
- Protein 68.6 g

Indian Roasted Chicken

Preparation Time: 10 minutes
Cooking Time: 45 minutes
Servings: 6

Ingredients:

- ¼ teaspoon ground cinnamon
- 4 garlic cloves, crushed
- ¾ teaspoon ground cumin
- ¼ teaspoon ground nutmeg
- 1 (3-pound) pasture-raised whole chicken
- ¾ teaspoon cayenne pepper
- ¼ teaspoon ground allspice
- ¼ teaspoon ground cloves
- ¾ teaspoon ground coriander
- Salt and freshly ground black pepper, to taste, to taste

Method:

1. Mix together all the spices in a bowl and rub the chicken in it.
2. Marinate and refrigerate for about 10 hours.
3. Preheat the oven to 510 degrees F and arrange a rack in a roasting pan.
4. Stuff the chicken cavity with garlic and place the chicken over rack.
5. Roast for about 15 minutes and decrease the temperature of oven to 435 degrees F.
6. Cover the chicken with pan drippings and roast for about 30 minutes.
7. Dish out and cut the chicken into desired slices.

Meal Prep Tip: Transfer the chicken slices onto a plate and keep aside to cool completely. Divide the chicken slices into 4 containers and cover them. Refrigerate for up to 5 days and reheat in the microwave before serving.

Nutritional Value:

- Calories 492
- Total Fat 34.6 g
- Saturated Fat 10.2 g
- Cholesterol 203 mg
- Total Carbs 3.2 g

- Dietary Fiber 0.3 g
- Sugar 0.1 g
- Protein 42.8 g

Thanksgiving Turkey

Preparation Time: 15 minutes
Cooking Time: 2 hours
Servings: 15
Ingredients:

- 1½ tablespoons fresh sage, chopped
- 2 teaspoons garlic, minced
- ½ cup olive oil
- 1½ tablespoons fresh thyme, chopped
- 1 (10-pound) whole turkey, neck and giblets removed
- Salt, to taste
- 2 tablespoons fresh rosemary, chopped

Method:

1. Preheat the oven to 340 degrees F and arrange a rack in a roasting pan.
2. Put the turkey in the roasting pan and transfer onto the rack.
3. Mix together all other ingredients in a small bowl and rub this mixture beneath the turkey skin.
4. Spread the remaining oil mixture on the top of the turkey skin.
5. Bake for about 2 hours and dish out from the oven.
6. Cut into desired sized pieces and serve.

Meal Prep Tip: Divide the turkey mixture evenly in 8 containers and refrigerate for about 3 days. Reheat in microwave before serving.

Nutritional Value:

- Calories 578
- Total Fat 42.8 g
- Saturated Fat 12 g
- Cholesterol 2821 mg
- Total Carbs 4.2 g
- Dietary Fiber 0.4 g
- Sugar 0 g
- Protein 41.5 g

MEAT RECIPES

Harvest Beef Salad

Preparation Time: 15 minutes
Cooking Time: 10 minutes
Servings: 6

Ingredients:
- 2 tablespoons extra-virgin olive oil, divided
- 1½ teaspoons organic honey
- 6 teaspoons fresh lemon juice, divided
- Salt and freshly ground black pepper, to taste
- 1½ pounds grass-fed flank steak, trimmed
- 10 cups fresh baby arugula
- 4 apples, cored and sliced thinly

Method:
1. Mix together 1 teaspoon of lemon juice, 1½ teaspoons of oil, salt and black pepper in a bowl and add steak.
2. Heat a non-stick skillet over medium high-heat and add beef.
3. Cook for about 5 minutes on each side and dish out the steak.
4. Cut the beef steak diagonally and add remaining lemon juice, oil, honey, sea salt and black pepper in a bowl.
5. Coat arugula in this mixture and divide arugula in serving plates.
6. Top with beef and apple slices evenly and serve.

Meal Prep Tip: Divide salad in 4 containers and refrigerate for about 1 day.

Nutritional Value:
- Calories 375
- Total Fat 17.4 g
- Saturated Fat 6.1 g
- Cholesterol 81 mg
- Total Carbs 23.3 g
- Dietary Fiber 4.2 g
- Sugar 17.7 g

- Protein 32.4 g

Bright Colored Beef Burgers

Preparation Time: 8 minutes
Cooking Time: 15 minutes
Servings: 4

Ingredients:
- ¾ medium beetroot, trimmed, peeled and chopped finely
- ¾ tablespoon fresh rosemary, chopped finely
- 1½ tablespoons olive oil
- ¾ pound grass-fed ground beef
- ¾ carrot, peeled and chopped finely
- ¾ small brown onion, chopped finely
- Salt and freshly ground black pepper, to taste

Method:
1. Mix together all the ingredients in a large bowl except oil.
2. Make equal sized patties from mixture and heat oil in a large skillet over medium heat.
3. Cook for about 4 minutes on each side and serve hot.

Meal Prep Tip: Remove the patties from heat and keep aside to cool completely. Store in an airtight container and in order to avoid the sticking, place parchment papers between the burgers. These burgers can be stored in refrigerator for about 1 day. Reheat in microwave before serving.

Nutritional Value:
- Calories 335
- Total Fat 27.7 g
- Saturated Fat 6.2 g
- Cholesterol 56 mg
- Total Carbs 4.4 g
- Dietary Fiber 1.1 g
- Sugar 2.4 g
- Protein 17.8 g

Family Dinner Pork Shoulder

Preparation Time: 15 minutes
Cooking Time: 6 hours
Servings: 9
Ingredients:
- ¼ cup fresh rosemary, minced
- 1 (3-pound) pork shoulder
- 6 garlic cloves, peeled and crushed
- 1 tablespoon fresh lemon juice
- 1 tablespoon balsamic vinegar

Method:
1. Mix together all the ingredients in a bowl except pork shoulder.
2. Put the pork shoulder in a large roasting pan and coat with marinade.
3. Cover with a plastic wrap and refrigerate for at least 2 hours to marinate well.
4. Keep the marinade at room temperature for 1 hour and preheat the oven to 275 degrees F.
5. Transfer the roasting pan in the oven and roast for about 6 hours.
6. Dish out and cut into desired slices to serve.

Meal Prep Tip: Transfer the pork slices into a large bowl and keep aside to cool completely. Divide the mixture into 6 containers evenly and cover the containers. Refrigerate for up to 4 days and reheat in the microwave before serving.

Nutritional Value:
- Calories 105
- Total Fat 0.3 g
- Saturated Fat 0 g
- Cholesterol 0 mg
- Total Carbs 25.8 g
- Dietary Fiber 5.6 g
- Sugar 19.2 g
- Protein 2.2 g

Hawaiian Pineapple Pork

Preparation Time: 15 minutes
Cooking Time: 20 minutes
Servings: 4

Ingredients:
- ¾ onion, chopped
- ¾ teaspoon fresh ginger, minced
- ¼ cup fresh pineapple juice
- 1½ tablespoons coconut oil
- 1-pound pork tenderloin, cut into bite-sized pieces
- 1½ garlic cloves, minced
- ¾ teaspoon red pepper flakes, crushed
- ounce fresh pineapple, cut into chunks
- Salt and freshly ground black pepper, to taste
- ¼ cup coconut aminos

Method:
1. Heat oil in a large skillet over medium heat and add pork.
2. Cook for about 5 minutes and dish out into a large bowl.
3. Put onions in the same skillet and sauté for about 5 minutes.
4. Stir in ginger, red pepper flakes and garlic and sauté for about 1 minute.
5. Add pineapple and cook for about 4 minutes.
6. Stir in coconut aminos, pineapple juice, cooked pork, salt and black pepper and cook for about 5 minutes.
7. Dish out and serve hot.

Meal Prep Tip: Transfer the pork pieces into a large bowl and keep aside to cool completely. Divide the mixture into 4 containers evenly and cover the containers. Refrigerate for up to 5 days and reheat in the microwave before serving.

Nutritional Value:
- Calories 451
- Total Fat 32.6 g
- Saturated Fat 12 g
- Cholesterol 136 mg

- Total Carbs 1.7 g
- Dietary Fiber 0.7 g
- Sugar 0.1 g
- Protein 35.4 g

Delish Lamb Chops

Preparation Time: 15 minutes
Cooking Time: 7 minutes
Servings: 6

Ingredients:
- 6 small garlic cloves, halved
- ¼ teaspoon red pepper flakes, crushed
- 1½ tablespoons fresh lemon juice
- 4 tablespoons fresh parsley, chopped finely and divided
- 2 tablespoons olive oil
- 8 (4-ounce) (½-inch thick) grass-fed lamb loin chops, trimmed
- ¼ teaspoon dried thyme, crushed
- Salt and freshly ground black pepper, to taste
- 4 tablespoons filtered water

Method:
1. Heat oil in a large skillet over medium-high heat and add garlic.
2. Sauté for about 1 minute and add thyme, chops, salt, red pepper flakes and black pepper.
3. Cook for about 3 minutes and flip the side.
4. Cook for another 3 minutes and divide the chops in serving plates.
5. Pour water, lemon juice and half of parsley and cook for about 1 minute, stirring continuously.
6. Drizzle the sauce evenly over chops and garnish with remaining parsley.

Meal Prep Tip: Divide the lamb chops evenly in 6 containers and refrigerate for about 3 days. Reheat in microwave before serving.

Nutritional Value:
- Calories 475
- Total Fat 39.5 g
- Saturated Fat 15.4 g
- Cholesterol 107 mg
- Total Carbs 1.3 g
- Dietary Fiber 0.2 g

- Sugar 0.1 g
- Protein 25.7 g

Prime Rib Roast

Preparation Time: 15 minutes
Cooking Time: 1 hour 30 minutes
Servings: 15

Ingredients:
- 20 garlic cloves, minced
- 1 (6-pound) grass-fed prime rib roast
- 3 teaspoons dried thyme, crushed
- 4 tablespoons olive oil
- Salt and freshly ground black pepper, to taste

Method:
1. Put all the ingredients in a large bowl except rib roast.
2. Put the rib roast in a large roasting pan and cover rib roast evenly with garlic mixture.
3. Marinate for at least 2 hours at room temperature and preheat the oven to 495 degrees F.
4. Roast for about 20 minutes and decrease the temperature to 325 degrees F.
5. Roast for about 70 minutes and dish out.
6. Cut the rib roast in desired slices and serve.

Meal Prep Tip: Transfer the rib roast slices into a large bowl and keep aside to cool completely. Divide the mixture into 4 containers evenly and cover the containers. Refrigerate for up to 5 days and reheat in the microwave before serving.

Nutritional Value:
- Calories 471
- Total Fat 36.2 g
- Saturated Fat 13.5 g
- Cholesterol 108 mg
- Total Carbs 3.6 g
- Dietary Fiber 0.2 g
- Sugar 0 g
- Protein 30.5 g

Beef and Cauliflower

Preparation Time: 15 minutes
Cooking Time: 15 minutes
Servings: 4

Ingredients:

- 1½ pounds grass-fed beef, cut into bite sized pieces
- 1½ tablespoons olive oil
- 6 garlic cloves, minced
- 4 cups small cauliflower florets
- 1½ tablespoons fresh lime juice
- ¾ teaspoon paprika, crushed
- 4 tablespoons coconut aminos
- Salt and freshly ground black pepper, to taste
- ¾ cup fresh basil leaves, finely chopped

Method:

1. Season the beef with a little salt and black pepper and keep aside.
2. Put olive oil in a large skillet over medium heat and add garlic and paprika.
3. Sauté for about 1 minute and enhance the heat to medium-high.
4. Add beef and cook for about 6 minutes.
5. Meanwhile, boil cauliflower in a pan and cook for about 5 minutes.
6. Drain the cauliflower florets and add the cauliflower and coconut aminos in the skillet.
7. Cook for about 3 minutes, rarely stirring and sprinkle salt, black pepper and lime juice.
8. Remove from heat and garnish with fresh basil leaves.

Meal Prep Tip: Transfer the beef mixture into a large bowl and keep aside to cool completely. Divide the mixture into 6 containers evenly and cover the containers. Refrigerate for up to 4 days and reheat in the microwave before serving.

Nutritional Value:

- Calories 407
- Total Fat 21.9 g
- Saturated Fat 7.5 g

- Cholesterol 113 mg
- Total Carbs 11.6 g
- Dietary Fiber 3.1 g
- Sugar 3 g
- Protein 37.8 g

Divine Leg of Lamb

Preparation Time: 15 minutes
Cooking Time: 1 hour 30 minutes
Servings: 10

Ingredients:

- 3 garlic cloves, minced
- ¾ teaspoon ground allspice
- 1 (4-pound) grass-fed leg of lamb, trimmed
- 1½ tablespoons ground coriander
- 1½ tablespoons smoked paprika
- ½ cup olive oil
- 3 teaspoons fresh lemon zest, grated finely
- 3 tablespoons ground cumin
- ½ cup fresh parsley, minced
- 3 tablespoons paprika, finely crushed

Method:

1. Put all the ingredients in a large bowl except leg of lamb.
2. Add leg of lamb and coat generously with marinade mixture.
3. Cover with a plastic wrap and refrigerate for about 8 hours.
4. For about 30 minutes, keep at room temperature.
5. Preheat the oven to 345 degrees F and grease a roasting pan.
6. Place a rack in the oven and transfer the leg of lamb over the rack.
7. Roast for about 1½ hours, flipping once in the half way.
8. Cut into desired slices and serve hot.

Meal Prep Tip: Transfer the lamb slices onto a wire rack to cool completely. Wrap the lamb slices with foil pieces and refrigerate for about 2 days. Reheat in the microwave before serving.

Nutritional Value:

- Calories 426
- Total Fat 22.7 g
- Saturated Fat 5.8 g
- Cholesterol 158 mg
- Total Carbs 2.1 g

- Dietary Fiber 0.8 g
- Sugar 0.2 g
- Protein 51.8 g

Superior Beef Tenderloin Roast

Preparation Time: 10 minutes
Cooking Time: 50 minutes
Servings: 6

Ingredients:

- 4 garlic cloves, minced
- 1 (2-pound) grass-fed center-cut beef tenderloin roast
- 1½ tablespoons fresh rosemary, minced and divided
- Salt and freshly ground black pepper, to taste
- ¾ tablespoon olive oil

Method:

1. Preheat the oven to 430 degrees F and grease a large roasting pan.
2. Rub the beef with the garlic, rosemary, salt and black pepper and drizzle with oil.
3. Transfer the beef into the prepared roasting pan and roast for about 50 minutes.
4. Dish out and cut the beef tenderloin in desired slices.

Meal Prep Tip: Transfer the beef slices into a large bowl and keep aside to cool completely. Divide the mixture into 6 containers evenly and cover the containers. Refrigerate for up to 4 days and reheat in the microwave before serving.

Nutritional Value:

- Calories 340
- Total Fat 17.5 g
- Saturated Fat 6.2 g
- Cholesterol 126 mg
- Total Carbs 1.2 g
- Dietary Fiber 0.4 g
- Sugar 0 g
- Protein 42.1 g

Mushroom Beef Steaks

Preparation Time: 15 minutes
Cooking Time: 30 minutes
Servings: 6

Ingredients:
- 3 scallions, chopped finely
- 6 (4-ounce) grass-fed T-bone steaks, trimmed
- 1½ pounds fresh button mushrooms, sliced
- 3 tablespoons fresh lemon juice
- Salt and freshly ground black pepper, to taste
- 1½ cups homemade chicken broth
- 3 tablespoons olive oil, divided
- 3 tablespoons fresh rosemary, chopped

Method:
1. Season the steaks with salt and black pepper and heat ½ tablespoon of oil in a non-stick skillet over medium-high heat.
2. Add steaks and cook for about 5 minutes on each side.
3. Transfer the steaks into a large bowl and cover with a piece of foil.
4. Heat remaining oil in the same skillet over medium heat and add rosemary and scallions.
5. Sauté for about 1 minute and add mushrooms.
6. Cook for about 8 minutes and add broth and lemon juice.
7. Bring to a gentle simmer and cook for about 4 minutes.
8. Stir in salt and black pepper and dish out steaks in serving plates.
9. Top with mushroom gravy and serve hot.

Meal Prep Tip: Transfer the steak mixture into a large bowl and keep aside to cool completely. Divide the mixture into 6 containers evenly and cover the containers. Refrigerate for up to 4 days and reheat in the microwave before serving.

Nutritional Value:
- Calories 328
- Total Fat 18.1 g
- Saturated Fat 5.1 g

- Cholesterol 60 mg
- Total Carbs 5.7 g
- Dietary Fiber 2.1 g
- Sugar 2.4 g
- Protein 36.1 g

CHAPTER 11: VEGETABLES RECIPES

Veggies-filled Mushrooms

Preparation Time: 25 minutes
Cooking Time: 1 hour
Servings: 6

Ingredients:
- 2 parsnips, peeled and chopped
- ¾ large onion, chopped and divided
- 1½ medium sweet potatoes, peeled and chopped
- 1/3 cup fresh rosemary, chopped
- 2 tablespoons coconut oil
- 2 large carrots, peeled and chopped
- 5 Portobello mushrooms, chopped
- ¼ teaspoon fresh cilantro, chopped
- Salt and freshly ground black pepper, to taste
- 3 medium garlic cloves, minced and divided
- 1¾ cups homemade vegetable broth

Method:
1. Preheat the oven to 375 degrees F and heat half of the oil in a large skillet over medium heat.
2. Add carrots, half of onion, half of garlic cloves, parsnips and sweet potato and sauté for about 5 minutes.
3. Transfer the veggie mixture evenly into a large casserole dish.
4. Heat remaining oil in another skillet over medium heat and add mushrooms, rosemary and remaining onions and garlic.
5. Sauté for about 5 minutes and stir in broth.
6. Bring to a boil and season with salt and black pepper.
7. Dish out and pour broth mixture over veggie mixture.
8. Bake for about 40 minutes and serve hot.

Meal Prep Tip: Transfer the veggies-filled mushrooms into a large bowl and keep aside to cool completely. Divide the mixture into 6 containers evenly and cover the containers. Refrigerate for about 2 days and reheat in the microwave before serving.

Nutritional Value:
- Calories 168
- Total Fat 5.2 g
- Saturated Fat 4.2 g
- Cholesterol 0 mg
- Total Carbs 28.5 g
- Dietary Fiber 7.2 g
- Sugar 4.9 g
- Protein 4.3 g

Citrus Brussels Sprout

Preparation Time: 15 minutes
Cooking Time: 15 minutes
Servings: 6

Ingredients:
- 1½ teaspoons paprika, crushed
- 6 garlic cloves, minced
- 6 tablespoons olive oil
- 2 tablespoons fresh lemon juice
- 1½ pounds Brussels sprouts, halved
- Salt and freshly ground black pepper, to taste

Method:
1. Arrange a steamer basket over a pan of boiling filtered water.
2. Place Brussels sprouts in steamer basket and steam for about 8 minutes.
3. Drain well and keep aside.
4. Put oil, garlic and paprika in a large skillet over medium heat and sauté for about 1 minute.
5. Add Brussels sprouts, sea salt and black pepper and sauté for about 5 minutes.
6. Stir in lemon juice and sauté for about 1 minute.

Meal Prep Tip: Transfer the Brussels sprouts into a large bowl and keep aside to cool completely. Divide the mixture into 6 containers evenly and cover the containers. Refrigerate for about 5 days and reheat in the microwave before serving.

Nutritional Value:
- Calories 176
- Total Fat 14.5 g
- Saturated Fat 2.2 g
- Cholesterol 0 mg
- Total Carbs 11.7 g
- Dietary Fiber 4.5 g
- Sugar 2.6 g
- Protein 4.2 g

Crispy Veggie Salad

Preparation Time: 15 minutes
Cooking Time: 0 minute
Servings: 6

Ingredients:

For Salad:
- 1½ cups baby arugula
- 2 cups green cabbage, shredded
- ¾ cup fresh parsley leaves, chopped
- 3 cups carrots, peeled and shredded
- 3 large scallions, chopped
- 2 cups Chinese cabbage, shredded

For Dressing:
- ¾ teaspoon fresh lemon zest, grated finely
- Salt and freshly ground black pepper, to taste
- 3 tablespoons fresh lemon juice
- 3 tablespoons extra virgin olive oil

Method:
1. Put all the salad ingredients in a large serving bowl and mix well.
2. Put all the dressing ingredients in another bowl and pour dressing over salad.
3. Toss to coat well and immediately serve.

Meal Prep Tip: Divide the dressing in the bottom of 6 large mason jars. Divide the salad ingredients in the layers and cover each jar with the lid tightly. Refrigerate for about 3 days and shake the jars well just before serving.

Nutritional Value:
- Calories 101
- Total Fat 7.2 g
- Saturated Fat 1.1 g
- Cholesterol 0 mg
- Total Carbs 9.1 g
- Dietary Fiber 2.9 g

- Sugar 4.4 g
- Protein 1.8 g

Hearty Broccoli

Preparation Time: 15 minutes
Cooking Time: 10 minutes
Servings: 6

Ingredients:

- 1½ tablespoons coconut oil
- 1½ pounds fresh broccoli florets
- 1½ tablespoons fresh ginger, minced
- 1½ teaspoons cumin seeds
- ¾ cup unsweetened coconut flakes
- 3 teaspoons curry powder
- Salt, to taste
- 3 tablespoons filtered water
- ¾ small yellow onion, sliced thinly

Method:

1. Heat a large non-stick skillet over medium heat and add coconut flakes.
2. Cook for about 4 minutes and dish out in a bowl.
3. Heat oil in the same skillet and add rest of the ingredients except broccoli.
4. Sauté for about 2 minutes and add water and broccoli.
5. Stir to combine and enhance the heat to medium-high.
6. Cover and cook for about 4 minutes.
7. Top with toasted coconut flakes and serve.

Meal Prep Tip: Transfer the broccoli into a large bowl and keep aside to cool completely. Divide the mixture into 6 small containers evenly and cover the containers. Refrigerate for about 1 week and reheat in the microwave before serving.

Nutritional Value:

- Calories 116
- Total Fat 7.1 g
- Saturated Fat 5.5 g
- Cholesterol 0 mg
- Total Carbs 12.1 g
- Dietary Fiber 4.7 g

- Sugar 2.4 g
- Protein 4.1 g

Sweet & Sour Kale

Preparation Time: 15 minutes
Cooking Time: 20 minutes
Servings: 6

Ingredients:

- 4 garlic cloves, minced
- 1½ tablespoons extra-virgin olive oil
- 4 pounds fresh kale, trimmed and chopped
- 1½ lemons, seeded sliced thinly
- ¾ cup scallions, chopped
- 1½ tablespoons organic honey
- 3 onions, chopped
- Salt and black pepper, to taste

Method:

1. Heat oil in a large skillet over medium heat and add lemon slices.
2. Cook for about 5 minutes and dish out the lemon slices.
3. Add onions and garlic in the same skillet and sauté for about 5 minutes.
4. Add kale, scallions, salt, black pepper and honey and cook for about 10 minutes.
5. Garnish with lemon slices and serve hot.

Meal Prep Tip: Transfer the kale into a large bowl and keep aside to cool completely. Divide the mixture into 3 large containers evenly and cover the containers. Refrigerate for about 4 days and reheat in the microwave before serving.

Nutritional Value:

- Calories 228
- Total Fat 3.6 g
- Saturated Fat 0.5 g
- Cholesterol 0 mg
- Total Carbs 44 g
- Dietary Fiber 6.5 g
- Sugar 7.3 g
- Protein 10.2 g

Cauliflower Patties

Preparation Time: 15 minutes
Cooking Time: 45 minutes
Servings: 4

Ingredients:
- ¾ large organic egg
- 1/3 teaspoon ground turmeric
- 1½ cups cauliflower, chopped
- ½ cup almond flour
- 1/3 teaspoon paprika
- ¾ cup onion, minced
- 1/3 cup fresh cilantro leaves, minced
- 1 teaspoon ground cumin
- 2 tablespoons olive oil
- 2 garlic cloves, minced
- ¾ cup fresh parsley, minced
- 1 tablespoon arrowroot flour
- Salt, to taste

Method:
1. Preheat the oven to 400 degrees F and grease a large baking sheet.
2. For patties: Add all the ingredients in a food processor except olive oil and pulse until well combined.
3. Make equal sized balls from the mixture and coat each ball with oil.
4. Press into a thick patty and transfer the patties onto baking sheet.
5. Bake for about 30 minutes and flip the patties carefully.
6. Bake for about another 15 minutes and serve hot.

Meal Prep Tip: Transfer the patties into a large bowl and keep aside to cool completely. Divide the mixture into 4 containers evenly and cover the containers. Refrigerate for about 5 days and reheat in the microwave before serving.

Nutritional Value:
- Calories 186
- Total Fat 14.9 g

- Saturated Fat 1.8 g
- Cholesterol 35 mg
- Total Carbs 9 g
- Dietary Fiber 3.5 g
- Sugar 2.1 g
- Protein 5.8 g

Colorful Beet Pesto

Preparation Time: 15 minutes
Cooking Time: 1 hour
Servings: 6

Ingredients:

For Pesto:
- 8 cups fresh basil leaves
- Salt and freshly ground black pepper, to taste
- 3 large garlic cloves, chopped
- 1/3 cup pine nuts, chopped roughly
- 1/3 cup extra-virgin olive oil

For Cooking:
- 3 tablespoons olive oil
- 6 cups fresh kale, chopped
- 6 medium beets, trimmed, peeled and spiralized with blade C

Method:
1. Preheat the oven to 430 degrees F and grease a large baking sheet.
2. Add all the pesto ingredients in a food processor except oil and pulse until smooth.
3. Add olive oil and process again and set aside.
4. Place beet in a prepared baking sheet and sprinkle with oil, sea salt and black pepper.
5. Roast for about 10 minutes and dish out in a large bowl.
6. Add kale and pesto and toss well.

Meal Prep Tip: Transfer the beet pesto into a large bowl and keep aside to cool completely. Divide the mixture into 6 containers evenly and cover the containers. Refrigerate for about 4 days and reheat in the microwave before serving.

Nutritional Value:
- Calories 231
- Total Fat 16.7 g
- Saturated Fat 2 g
- Cholesterol 0 mg
- Total Carbs 18.8 g
- Dietary Fiber 3.6 g

- Sugar 7.2 g
- Protein 5.8 g

Tropical Fruity Salad

Preparation Time: 15 minutes
Cooking Time: 0 minute
Servings: 4

Ingredients:
- 2 tablespoons fresh lime juice
- 1½ fresh mangoes, peeled, pitted and cubed
- 6 cups fresh collards
- 1½ fresh papaya, peeled, seeded and cubed
- ¼ cup fresh mint leaves, chopped
- ¾ pound fresh pineapples, peeled and cut into chunks

Method:
1. Put all the ingredients in a large bowl except collards and toss to coat well.
2. Cover and refrigerate for at least 1 hour.
3. Divide collards onto serving plates and top with salad.

Meal Prep Tip: Divide salad in 4 containers and refrigerate for about 1 day.

Nutritional Value:
- Calories 193
- Total Fat 1.2 g
- Saturated Fat 0.3 g
- Cholesterol 0 mg
- Total Carbs 48.2 g
- Dietary Fiber 7.7 g
- Sugar 35.4 g
- Protein 3.7 g

CHAPTER 12: DESSERTS RECIPES

Pumpkin Brownies

Preparation Time: 15 minutes
Cooking Time: 45 minutes
Servings: 8

Ingredients:

- ¾ teaspoon powdered stevia
- ¾ cup unsweetened salted almond butter
- 8 tablespoons cacao powder
- 1½ cups homemade pumpkin puree

Method:

1. Preheat the oven to 350 degrees F and grease a loaf pan.
2. Put all the ingredients in a bowl and beat with an electric mixer.
3. Place the mixture into prepared loaf pan and flatten the surface.
4. Bake for about 45 minutes and dish out.
5. Cut into 8 equal sized brownies and serve.

Meal Prep Tip: Wrap each brownie piece into wax paper pieces. Place the wrapped brownies into an airtight container. Preserve at room temperature for about 4 days.

Nutritional Value:

- Calories 180
- Total Fat 14.9 g
- Saturated Fat 1.9 g
- Cholesterol 0 mg
- Total Carbs 11.6 g
- Dietary Fiber 3.5 g
- Sugar 2.7 g
- Protein 5.3 g

Strawberries Chia Seeds Pudding

Preparation Time: 15 minutes
Cooking Time: 0 minute
Servings: 6

Ingredients:
- 3 cups unsweetened almond milk
- 1½ teaspoons organic vanilla extract
- 1½ (16-ounce) packages fresh strawberries, hulled and sliced
- ¾ cup chia seeds
- ¾ cup organic honey

Method:
1. Put almond milk and strawberries in a food processor and pulse until smooth.
2. Dish out the mixture in a bowl and add rest of the ingredients.
3. Stir well to combine and refrigerate, covered to chill for about 3 hours.

Meal Prep Tip: Transfer the pudding into a large serving bowl and keep aside to cool completely. Cover the bowl with plastic wraps and refrigerate for about 1 day.

Nutritional Value:
- Calories 205
- Total Fat 3.2 g
- Saturated Fat 0.3 g
- Cholesterol 0 mg
- Total Carbs 46.3 g
- Dietary Fiber 4.1 g
- Sugar 40.5 g
- Protein 2 g

Grilled Peaches

Preparation Time: 10 minutes
Cooking Time: 14 minutes
Servings: 8

Ingredients:
- ¼ teaspoon ground cinnamon
- 2 fresh medium peaches, halved and pitted
- ¼ cup chilled coconut cream, whipped
- 1½ teaspoons organic vanilla extract

Method:
1. Preheat the grill to medium-high heat and grease the grill grate.
2. Arrange the peaches onto prepared grill and grill for about 7 minutes per side.
3. Put vanilla extract and coconut cream in a bowl and beat until well combined.
4. Top each peach piece with whipped coconut cream and dust with cinnamon.

Meal Prep Tip: Transfer the grilled peaches into a large serving bowl and keep aside to cool completely. Cover the bowl with plastic wraps and refrigerate for about 3 days.

Nutritional Value:
- Calories 69
- Total Fat 5.1 g
- Saturated Fat 4.1 g
- Cholesterol 0 mg
- Total Carbs 5.3 g
- Dietary Fiber 0.7 g
- Sugar 3.6 g
- Protein 0.9 g

Blueberry Cake

Preparation Time: 10 minutes
Cooking Time: 5 minutes
Servings: 6

Ingredients:
- 6 teaspoons organic honey
- 3 cups fresh blueberries, blended with 2 teaspoons water
- 6 large organic eggs, beaten lightly
- 1 teaspoon organic baking powder
- 1 teaspoon ground cinnamon
- 6 tablespoons unsweetened almond milk
- 3 tablespoons raw walnuts, chopped
- 12 tablespoons almond flour
- Pinch of salt

Method:
1. Put all the ingredients in a mug and mix well.
2. Microwave for about 5 minutes and keep aside.
3. Serve warm.

Meal Prep Tip: Carefully invert the cake onto a wire rack to cool completely. Wrap cake slices with plastic sheets and then place the wrapped layers in a plastic zip lock bag. Store for up to 5 days on the kitchen counter at room temperature.

Nutritional Value:
- Calories 247
- Total Fat 14.4 g
- Saturated Fat 2.2 g
- Cholesterol 186 mg
- Total Carbs 20.9 g
- Dietary Fiber 3.8 g
- Sugar 13.4 g
- Protein 10.9 g

Chocolate Mousse

Preparation Time: 15 minutes
Cooking Time: 2 minutes
Servings: 10
Ingredients:

- 1½ teaspoons instant coffee
- 4 tablespoons coconut oil
- 4 tablespoons cacao powder
- 8 Medjool dates, pitted and chopped
- 1½ teaspoons organic vanilla extract
- ounce 75% dark chocolate, chopped
- ¾ cup unsweetened coconut milk
- 6 large ripe avocados, peeled, pitted and chopped
- 6 tablespoons organic honey

Method:

1. Mix together cacao powder, coconut oil, coffee and chocolate in a large microwave-safe bowl and microwave for about 2 minutes.
2. Put the remaining ingredients in a food processor and pulse until smooth.
3. Add chocolate mixture and pulse until creamy and smooth.
4. Transfer the mousse in serving bowls and refrigerate, covered for about 3 hours.

Meal Prep Tip: Place the mousse into an airtight container and preserve in refrigerator for up to 4 days.

Nutritional Value:

- Calories 374
- Total Fat 29.8 g
- Saturated Fat 13.2 g
- Cholesterol 0 mg
- Total Carbs 29.3 g
- Dietary Fiber 9.2 g
- Sugar 17.1 g
- Protein 3.8 g

Strawberry Custard

Preparation Time: 10 minutes
Cooking Time: 25 minutes
Servings: 6

Ingredients:
- ¾ teaspoon organic vanilla extract
- 3 organic eggs
- 10-ounce unsweetened coconut milk
- 1½ cup strawberries, peeled and mashed finely

Method:
1. Preheat the oven to 350 degrees F and grease 6 (6-inch) custard cups.
2. Arrange the glasses in a large baking dish.
3. Put all the ingredients in a large bowl and mix well.
4. Divide the strawberry mixture in prepared custard cups and pour in the baking dish.
5. Bake for about 25 minutes and dish out to serve.

Meal Prep Tip: Transfer the custard into a large serving bowl and keep aside to cool completely. Cover the bowl with plastic wraps and refrigerate for about 1 day.

Nutritional Value:
1. Calories 153
2. Total Fat 13.6 g
3. Saturated Fat 10.7 g
4. Cholesterol 82 mg
5. Total Carbs 5.6 g
6. Dietary Fiber 1.8 g
7. Sugar 3.6 g
8. Protein 4.1 g

Berry Granita

Preparation Time: 15 minutes
Cooking Time: 0 minute
Servings: 8

Ingredients:

- 3 tablespoons fresh lemon juice
- 1½ cups fresh blueberries
- 1½ cups fresh raspberries
- 3 cups ice cubes, crushed
- 3 cups fresh strawberries, hulled and sliced
- 3 tablespoons organic honey
- 3 teaspoons fresh mint leaves

Method:

1. Put all the ingredients in a high-speed blender except mint leaves and pulse until smooth.
2. Transfer into a baking dish and freeze for at least 30 minutes.
3. Remove from freezer and mix the granita with a fork.
4. Freeze for about 1 hour and garnish with mint leaves.
5. Serve chilled.

Meal Prep Tip: Transfer the granita into a large serving bowl and refrigerate for about 4 days.

Nutritional Value:

- Calories 70
- Total Fat 0.5 g
- Saturated Fat 0.1 g
- Cholesterol 0 mg
- Total Carbs 17.5 g
- Dietary Fiber 3.3 g
- Sugar 13 g
- Protein 0.9 g

Dark Chocolate Fudge

Preparation Time: 15 minutes
Cooking Time: 4 minutes
Servings: 6

Ingredients:
- ¾ cup 75% dark chocolate chips
- 1/3 cup unsalted, natural creamy almond butter

Method:
1. Put almond butter and chocolate chips in a microwave-safe bowl and microwave for 4 minutes on high.
2. Place the mixture onto a loaf pan lined with parchment paper and flatten the surface.
3. Freeze for about 1 hour and cut into equal squares.

Meal Prep Tip: Wrap each fudge piece into wax paper pieces and place into a resealable bag. Freeze for up to 3 weeks and remove from the freezer. Keep at room temperature for about 4 minutes before serving.

Nutritional Value:
- Calories 114
- Total Fat 10.1 g
- Saturated Fat 1.9 g
- Cholesterol 0 mg
- Total Carbs 4.8 g
- Dietary Fiber 0.9 g
- Sugar 1.8 g
- Protein 2.5 g

CONCLUSION

Lectins are mostly present in the seeds of the plants and are considered to be harmful. There is also a considerable amount of research supporting the role of plant foods in our body despite the fact that they are considered harmful. According to varying types of the plants the lectins levels may vary from plant to plant. The research that has been carried out on lentils has mostly been performed on the animals and test tube studies. Lectins have been credited with the many medical complications and the diseases like inflammation and digestion issues despite of the fact that researchers have focused on a specific lectin rather than the plants carrying it as a whole. Meal prepping in combination with lectin free diet provides us with both quick and nutritious food. Now, lectin free foods can be prepared and stored, then can be used instantly when required.

Made in the USA
San Bernardino, CA
13 November 2018